# Tales and Testaments

## The Art of Inspiring Storytelling

# Table of Contents

# Chapter 1. Introduction

Welcome, dear reader, to a mesmerizing journey through the realm of the spoken and written word! Our special report, "Tales and Testaments: The Art of Inspiring Storytelling," is a jubilant sojourn through centuries of enchanting narratives and poignant tales. This magical expedition doesn't only review the history of compelling storytelling, but it delves into the craft itself, unraveling the tapestry of techniques that make stories come alive. We firmly believe that everyone has a story within them, waiting for the right wand stroke to spark it into life; this report is your enchanted map to lead the way. We invite you to embark on this voyage with us, ready to inspire and be inspired. This report isn't just for sale, it's an investment in the timeless skill of storytelling, an empowering asset that can be yours today!

# Chapter 2. The Allure of Ancient Tales

Ever since the dawn of civilization, myths, legends, and tales have been the lifeblood of our culture, coursing through our collective consciousness, enchanting the minds of both young and old. Venerable literatures left by ancestors have served not only as a window into their time, but also as mirrors reflecting our present and guides illuminating our future. To unravel the allure of these ancient tales, we must first venture into the mythical narrative's origin and evolution, then explore the elements that make these compelling.

## 2.1. A Journey Through Time: The Evolution of Ancient Tales

Humankind's storytelling tradition was born out of necessity – the primal need to communicate, to share experiences, and to understand the universe. Early humans, huddled in caves, painted their stories on the walls – their trials, triumphs, and dreams. More than just an artistic endeavor, it was their mode of conveying collective wisdom and shared history.

As civilizations grew, so did the complexity of their narratives. The Sumerians etched theirs in cuneiform on clay tablets. The Egyptians painted and chiseled their tales on the walls of their colossal pyramids and majestic temples. These were the birth pangs of what we now know as literary art.

Ancient epics like "The Epic of Gilgamesh," "The Iliad," "The Odyssey," and "The Mahabharata" are shining examples of ancient storytelling. Rich in morality, exploration of human nature, and the pursuit of immortality, these tales fascinate us with their complexity, depth, and timeless themes.

## 2.2. The Threads that Weave the Tapestry: Elements of Alluring Ancient Tales

Ancient tales are no mere concatenation of events. They are a rich interplay of elements that blend together to create enchanting narratives that continue to captivate us even after thousands of years.

Narrative structure plays a crucial role in shaping the allure of ancient tales. These stories often follow patterns and structures – the heroic journey or the cycle of nature. This rhythm and predictability create a timeless and universal resonance.

Archetypical characters, another key element, strike a chord with us due to their familiarity. The valiant hero, the wise old sage, the cunning trickster, the nurturing mother - these characters are found across cultures, embodying universal human experiences and emotions.

Ancient tales also employ vivid imagery and metaphorical language. Imagery served as the language's brush strokes, painting a vivid picture of the narrative in the audience's mind. Classical metaphors and allegories masked profound wisdom under simple allegories and parables, slowly revealing their depth as one delves further.

## 2.3. Cultural Signatures: Ancient Tales as a Reflection of Societies

Furthermore, ancient tales tell as much about the societies that created them as they do about their direct subject matter. They are cultural fingerprints, enduring symbols of antiquated civilizations. The value systems, religious beliefs, societal structures – all are reflected in these narratives, offering us a glimpse into their world.

Ancient Greek mythology, a veritable pantheon of gods and heroes, mirrored the Greeks' valorization of human excellence and achievement. Norse myths, with their epic battles and somber destinies, resonated with the volatile, unpredictable nature of life in harsh Scandinavian climates.

# 2.4. Ancient Tales: An Enduring Legacy

In conclusion, the allure of ancient tales lies not just in the narratives themselves, but in the timeless wisdom they contain. They provide countless generations with a wealth of timeless virtues and values that still resonate in our world today. Their themes continue to define the human condition – love, sacrifice, betrayal, honor, courage – universal concepts that transcend cultures, time, and space.

The ability to appreciate these enchanting tales requires the willingness to venture beyond the literal surface of the narrative, to explore the layers beneath. Each word, each character, each twist of the plot is a piece of a grand puzzle, waiting for us, the readers, to put together.

These tales are a testament to our ancestors' creativity, wisdom, and their timeless urge to navigate the human condition's challenges. They are the elixirs that have nourished our collective imagination and will continue to do so for generations to come. Their allure lies in their enduring relevance, their ability to inspire, uplift, caution, and connect us across the chasm of time.

# Chapter 3. Understanding the Anatomy of a Story

In grasping the anatomy of a narrative, we take a microscope to the intricate components that make a story beat with life and meaning. A story, much like a living organism, depends on the essential structure and the relationships between its components to function effectively.

Let's begin with the simplest component, which forms the basic building block of any narrative – a moment captured in ink.

# Chapter 4. The Moment

The moment is a component of a narrative that depicts a single event or circumstance in time. It's a fleeting glimpse, a warp in the fabric of the narrative that offers a glimpse into a particular situation, location, and character interaction.

For example, consider the statement: "Alex opened the creaky gate leading to the haunted mansion late at night". This sentence is a moment - it captures a specific event at a particular time.

# Chapter 5. Scenes: A Sequence of Moments

Then we progress to 'scenes'. A scene is a narrative unit that contains connected events. It plays out a sequence of those atomic events or 'moments', typically involving characters and action, happening within a single location or a series of closely connected settings.

Following our previous example, Alex, after opening the creaky gate, might slowly explore the haunted mansion, confronting his fears as the ominous shadows grow taller with each step. This entire sequence forms a scene.

Creating an engaging scene is vital to any story. The creative application of detail, emotion, and pacing can make your scene imprint in the reader's memory.

Tip: Always make sure that each scene serves a purpose. It should either advance the plot, reveal something new about our characters, or open up new ideas and themes.

# Chapter 6. Sequences: Connected Scenes

A step above scenes, we encounter 'sequences'. A sequence is a series of connected scenes that collectively communicate a larger event or segment of the narrative. A sequence might explore a complete day in the life of the protagonist, the unfolding of a massive battle, or the hero's journey through a perilous forest.

In our haunted mansion journey, a sequence may include Alex exploring the house, confronting a ghost, and finally finding a hidden treasure. Each scene within this sequence moves the plot forward and fosters depth and complexity in the narrative.

# Chapter 7. Acts: The Pillars of Narrative

A lot higher in the hierarchy are 'Acts'. Acts represent the largest building blocks of your story—think of them as massive pillars holding up the narrative structure. Traditionally, most stories are crafted in three acts – the setup, confrontation, and resolution.

In our haunted mansion narrative, the first act might be Alex hearing rumors about the fortune and deciding to explore, the second act could be his terrifying and perilous quest inside the mansion, and the final act might depict his narrow escape with or without the treasure.

Remember, acts give your narrative structure. As an author, you decide how many acts your narrative includes, but traditionally three acts suffice. Each act should build on the momentum of the previous one and pivot into the next with an interesting turn of events, creating an engaging story.

Now that we've understood the basic structural hierarchy of a narrative let's look into the other vital elements that bring it to life – plot, character, theme, setting, and style.

## 7.1. Plot: The Path Through Your Story

The plot is essentially the sequence of interconnected events that make up your story. I often like to consider a plot like a path through the forest. It could be a straight path from start to finish or a winding trail offering multiple detours. Regardless, your plot should guide your reader just as a path guides a traveler, making each turn of the page another step along the journey.

In our haunted mansion story, the plot can be as straightforward or complex as we choose to make it. Will Alex find the treasure? Is there a twist of betrayal? Does a supernatural ally assist him? We form a basic structure and enhance it with unexpected developments and surprise elements that keep our readers engaged.

Also, a plot isn't necessarily linear. Some stories might start in present and flashback to the past, or they could start at the end and backtrack to how it all began. The author has complete discretion here.

# Chapter 8. Characters: The Heart of Your Story

Characters are representing figures through whom the reader witnesses the story unfold. They are the beating heart of your narrative, adding life and depth to an otherwise skeleton of a plot.

A character could be anyone, a brave lionhearted hero or a clever, deceptive antagonist, a supporting friend, or even a trusty old pet dog. A well-drawn character is one who is relatable and drives an emotional response from the reader. For instance, a reader might cheer for Alex rooting for his bravery and valor as he explores the haunted mansion.

Remember, characters should develop over the course of the story, and this development helps to drive the narrative forward.

# Chapter 9. Theme: The Underlying Message

Themes are the underlying ideas or messages conveyed through your story. The dominating themes in a narrative often relate to life, society, human nature-- essentially, the state of existence and being.

In our haunted mansion example, themes could include bravery, the human spirit's resilience, the struggle between good and evil, or even the consequences of greed.

Increasingly, authors are expanding to themes spanning social justice, mental health, and environmental issues.

# Chapter 10. Setting: The Stage of Your Story

The setting of your story is the environment where your narrative takes place. It can span whole galaxies in science fiction, the depths of the jungle, the bustling city streets or our humble haunted mansion.

A well-defined setting can serve as an immersive backdrop, helping your readers visualize the unfolding narrative. Not just a passive landscape, a setting can be an active element in your story, influencing the plot and character development with its inherent challenges and characteristics.

# Chapter 11. Style: Your Signature on Every Page

Lastly, we delve into 'style'. Each author's style is unique, like their signature. It is seen in the choices we make in our storytelling - the words we use, the sentence structure, the rhythm and pacing of our narrative, the use of imagery, and a lot more.

Your style can make your narrative distinctive. Think of the works of Charles Dickens, Ernest Hemingway, or J.K. Rowling; each has a unique style that resonates throughout their stories. So as you develop your narrative, explore your authentic voice and style.

Now, as we understand the elements that constitute a story, believe that each story you write will differ in their configuration. You decide how many acts to have, how your plot will unwind, who your characters are, and what themes naturally emerge. Not to forget, the setting and your unique style will seal the individuality of your story.

In this voyage through the anatomy of a narrative, you have been equipped with an understanding of how to build your story layer by layer, piece by piece. And this understanding serves as your guide, your compass in the art of storytelling.

Next, we'll venture into the realms of character creation, uncovering the nuances shaping unforgettable characters that leap off the page. It's time to step into their shoes, peer through their eyes, and breathe life into the hearts of these beings born from the marriage of ink and imagination.

But that, dear reader, is a tale for another chapter.

# Chapter 12. The Power of an Engaging Protagonist

Every tale is marked by its individuals, the social characters that lead us on magical expeditions through their thoughts, feelings, and experiences. The protagonist, being the primary figure, holds the capacity to attract us into their world, to walk in their shoes, and to feel their victories, sorrows, and growth. This chapter explores the power of an engaging protagonist and provides insight into crafting them to enhance the impact of our stories.

## 12.1. Crafting a Relatable Protagonist

The essence of an engaging protagonist is relatability. Readers should be able to identify with the character's motivations, struggles, and desires. This connection fosters investment in their journey, sparking emotions that resonate well beyond the confines of the book's pages.

Creating a relatable protagonist involves developing a background that informs their actions and choices. Birthplace, upbringing, family dynamics, education – all these elements shape character, providing dimensions that can mirror real human complexities. A reader might not have to share a protagonist's backstory to find them relatable; pain, joy, fear, ambition - these are universal emotions that traverse our disparate backgrounds.

Moreover, flawed protagonists offer the most compelling narratives. Perfection is both unreal and unrelatable for most individuals. True humanity lies in our imperfections – our struggles, our downfalls, our flaws, and our subsequent rise and transformation. Creating a protagonist who exhibits these attributes not only adds depth to the character but also fosters empathy and investment from your audience.

## 12.2. Protagonist Goals and Motivations

Every protagonist requires a goal, a destination or aspiration that serves as the driving force behind their actions. Crafting this appropriately involves careful thought and pertinence to the oeuvre of your narrative. Goals can present themselves in diverse ways, from saving a loved one to achieving a lifelong dream.

However, goals alone won't suffice. They must be underpinned by genuine motivations that push the protagonist towards their objective. For instance, a protagonist's goal might be to win a martial arts tournament, but their motivation would be their desire to honor their deceased mentor or to prove their self-worth. These motivations bind the audience with the protagonist, creating an emotional investment in their journey.

## 12.3. Encouraging Character Growth

An engaging protagonist is one that evolves, presenting character growth that aligns with the narrative. As the story unravels, the protagonist should experience situations that challenge them, confront their fears, and modify their perspectives. This transformation makes their journey believable and satisfying, signifying the narrative's impact on the character.

Consider employing a mixture of external and internal conflicts to stimulate character development. External conflicts evolve from physical challenges and interpersonal struggles, pushing the protagonist to outgrow their previous self. On the other hand, internal conflicts manifest from the protagonist's emotional turmoils, personal fears, and deep-seated insecurities. Both these conflicts, woven seamlessly into your narrative, nurture visceral character growth, deepening their engagement with the audience.

## 12.4. Creating Engaging Dialogue

Arguably, dialogue is one of the most potent tools in bringing your protagonist to life. A well-crafted dialogue does more than just share information; it divulges the protagonist's personality, their perspectives, and emotions. A fiery reply might exhibit courage; an empathetic response, kindness; a conflicted monologue, inner turmoil.

However, creating engaging dialogue entails authenticity. The language, tone, and pacing should align with the character's background, personality, and the situation. It should reveal, often subtly, their desires, fears, and struggles – adding layers to their personality and piquing the readers' interest with the depth it offers.

## 12.5. Balancing Agency and Vulnerability

An engaging protagonist exerts agency, influencing the narrative through actions, responses, decisions, and reflections. A passive protagonist who lets things happen to them rather than impacting the narrative's flow can dull the story, often leaving the readers uninvested.

Simultaneously, displaying vulnerability can make your protagonist more engaging, humanizing them in a way that readers can empathize with. Balancing these aspects—agency and vulnerability—can, therefore, create a more nuanced and impactful protagonist.

In conclusion, an engaging protagonist acts as the story's heart, beating with emotions, intentions, and actions that shape the story.

Crafting compelling protagonists necessitates an intricate blend of relatability, goal-oriented motivations, character growth, engaging dialogue, and a balanced agency-vulnerability combo. By mastering these aspects, one can breathe life into their protagonist, enchanting readers and anchoring them firmly within the narrative's magnetic pull.

# Chapter 13. The Crucial Role of Conflict and Resolution

Storytelling revolves around one central tenet: at the heart of every tale, be it whispered around a fireside or typed on a computer by a best-selling author, there's always a conflict, a struggle, a predicament. It's this point of tension that draws us in, making us personally invested in the outcome of the story, urging us to turn the page until the story reaches its resolution. Our exploration of storytelling, therefore, must invariably begin with a deep dive into the crucial role of conflict and resolution.

Let's start by demystifying conflict; contrarily to what it may imply, it isn't necessarily about a battle or a fight. Conflict, within the realm of storytelling, hones in on a roadblock, a hurdle, or a challenge that the protagonist must overcome. It's that knot that needs untangling, the shadow that needs a touch of light.

## 13.1. Defining Conflict and Resolution

Conflict is essentially the engine that drives a story, propelling characters into wrestling with their circumstances. It often takes the shape of one of these four types: character versus character, character versus nature, character versus society, or character versus self.

On the other hand, resolution, also known as denouement, is the "untangling" of the plot's complications and the story's final unraveling. It's the conclusion of the narrative—the point when all questions and quandaries find their answers, leaving the audience with a sense of completion and often an emotional response.

## 13.2. Nature of Conflict in Storytelling

Quite like a heartbeat keeps a body going, conflict injects momentum into a story. It elevates a mere chronicle of events into an emotionally charged journey, and in doing so, it engages emotions, stirs curiosity, and evokes empathy.

Moreover, conflict serves a more profound purpose—it questions the status quo, challenges norms, and thus paves the way for new thoughts, ideas, and actions. By portraying a character's stride through struggle, we inspire empathy, a sense of justice, disgust for injustice—basically a gamut of sentiments that make us human.

## 13.3. The Role of Conflict in Character Development

An untested character, like an untempered sword, lacks the strength and resilience that make them truly memorable. Conflict thrusts characters into challenging situations, and it's their reaction to these situations that, in turn, shapes their character, defining their qualities and flaws, their strengths, and weaknesses.

Through conflict, we witness the protagonist's endearing vulnerability, tenacious spirit, or even misguided motivations, each aspect adding layers to their character. Conflict, simply stated, is a crucible in which a character's true nature and dynamism are forged.

## 13.4. Anatomy of Resolution

The resolution is the required release following the tension-filled climb of the story arc, the unraveled knot that allows for a satisfying end. It doesn't have to be a 'happily ever after' or a perfectly tied bow—often, the best resolutions mirror life in their complexity and unpredictability.

A resolution could affirm the protagonist's actions, demonstrate their growth, or serve a hefty dose of poetic justice. Irrespective of its nature, the resolution should wrap up the loose ends, answer any lingering questions, and grant the reader relief from the story's built-up tension.

## 13.5. Resolution and Emotional Catharsis

The resolution also serves an additional purpose—providing a sense of emotional catharsis. This term, borrowed from the world of Greek drama, refers to the release of strong or repressed emotions. Whether it invokes tears of joy or sorrow, sighs of relief or frustration, the resolution must evoke a response, making the journey memorable and worthwhile.

## 13.6. Crafting Effective Conflict and Resolution

Using the right blend of conflict and resolution in a story is an art. To create engaging conflict, make your characters want something they can't easily get, or put them in situations that test their belief system or morality. And remember, a well-designed conflict should always align with the story's core theme and the protagonist's character arc.

As for resolution, it should be compelling and decisive. It shouldn't leave the audience hanging unless, of course, you're crafting a cliffhanger for a sequel. It should also showcase character development, illuminating the lessons learned and the transformations undergone by the characters throughout their ordeal.

In conclusion, the dance of conflict and resolution is indeed the lifeblood of any narrative. Skillfully implementing these elements can convert a simple story into a riveting tale, casting a spell that keeps the audience hooked till the very end. Embracing conflict can make your characters more relatable and human, while well-crafted resolutions can etch your story into the hearts and minds of your readers, leaving them moved, thoughtful, and eager for more.

# Chapter 14. Finding Your Voice: The Impact of Narrative Perspective

Throughout the annals of literature, narratives have always held the power to showcase the essence of human experience in its myriad forms. When articulated with finesse, each word, phrase, sentence, and paragraph dovetails into the next, producing a symphonic rhapsody that enthralls and sustains the reader's engagement. The fuel that fires the engine of this riveting narrative is the elusive yet potent force of 'voice'. This chapter delves into the fertile territory of narrative voice, laying bare its potential to shape narratives and stir souls.

## 14.1. The Essence of Voice

'Voice' in a narrative context is a unique blend of tone, style, rhythm, and intention brought together to breathe life into a text. The voice of a story can be as varied as the human vocal range and can dramatically influence how a story is received and interpreted. It could be authoritative, whimsical, critical, lyrical, get-under-your-skin confessional, or subtly persuasive.

## 14.2. Personal vs. Impersonal Voice

The narrative voice can either be personal or impersonal. A personal voice delves deep into the emotions, thoughts, and experiences of a character, often employing the first-person perspective for enhanced intimacy. On the other hand, the impersonal voice keeps a measured distance from the emotions and subjectivity of the characters, often found in third-person narrations with an omnipresent, detached narratorial perspective.

Choosing between a personal and impersonal voice depends on the story's needs and the intended impact on the audience. The personal voice draws readers into the internal life of the character and encourages empathy and emotional connection. In contrast, the impersonal voice, though emotionally detached, provides a more comprehensive overview of the plot, setting, and all involved characters, enabling a broader perspective.

# 14.3. Establishing a Consistent Voice

Consistency is significant in maintaining an effective narrative voice. Once a writer has chosen either a personal or impersonal voice, maintaining that voice throughout the storytelling journey is crucial. Consistency in voice fosters trust between the writer and the reader, smoothing the terrain for the reader's imaginative engagement.

An inconsistent voice can create confusion and distraction, diluting the story's potency. However, with practice, observation, and a keen ear for the nuances of effective narration, writers can cultivate the art of consistent voicing.

# 14.4. The Art of Modulation

While consistency matters, it is equally important to understand the art of modulation. An effective narrative voice should be flexible enough to adapt to the shifting moods, circumstances, and rhythms of a story without surrendering its distinguishable features.

Consider the example of a musical instrument. While the basic tone quality remains unaltered, playing different tunes requires the player to modulate that tone to match the music's needs. Similarly, a narrative voice needs the capability of modulation. It should be able to whisper and holler, laugh and sob, question and assert, all without losing its unique essence.

# 14.5. The Role of Perspective

Perspective can profoundly shape the narrative voice. First-person narration often employs a personal voice, capturing the character's internal thoughts, feelings, and perceptions, thus creating a highly subjective narrative. Third-person narration can embrace both personal and impersonal voice, with varying degrees of distance from the characters. Meanwhile, second-person narration, though rarer, involves the reader directly, using "you" as the primary pronoun.

Careful contemplation about the perspective that best serves your story can pave the way towards finding the fitting narrative voice. Remember, the perspective doesn't just decide who tells the story but also influences how your story is told and perceived.

# 14.6. The Experimentation With Voice

Experimenting with narrative voices can unveil surprising revelations about your storytelling style. It can help you unveil a voice that you never knew you had, or it can enhance a voice you've already developed.

Here are some practical strategies for experimentation:

1. Start by rewriting a single scene from your story in several different narrative voices.

2. Amplify or minimize emotional intensity in various versions.

3. Try telling the scene from different characters' perspectives.

4. Experiment with various blendings of personal and impersonal voice.

By doing so, writers can establish both the reach and limitations of their narrative voice, thus acting as a stepping stone for their growth as storytellers.

# 14.7. Conclusion: The Harmony of Craft and Voice

Every story purrs with an undercurrent of individuality that can be intriguing, gripping, or heartwarming. Understanding the mysteries of narrative voice and using them effectively largely determines if that undercurrent will break surface to breathe life into the words or remain buried within layers of text. Like unruly magic waiting for the right wand stroke, the narrative voice patiently hovers under every writer's fingertips, waiting to unfurl its potential in service of a captivating tale. With persistent craft, conscious choices, and playful experimentation, anyone can hone their narrative voice into a powerful storytelling agent. Further, the depth and nuance added through narrative perspective can provide additional fluidity and interest. Combine these elements together, and even the most experienced wordsmiths will stand in awe of your storytelling prowess.

# Chapter 15. Mastering the Art of Dialogue

Narrative dialogue serves as a potent tool in storytelling, affording characters their unique voices, and providing readers richer insights into their feelings, personalities, and relationships. A well-crafted dialogue can shape the plot, concretize the setting, and even communicate the underlying themes of the story.

## 15.1. Understanding the Purpose of Dialogue

When handled adeptly, the dialogue empowers characters to express themselves, lending authenticity to their thoughts, feelings, and motivations. Indeed, it is the lifeblood of any earthly situation or celestial scenario that we endeavor to pen. But to weave dialogue effortlessly into your work, an understanding of its fundamental purpose is essential.

Primarily, dialogue serves five main functions:

1. Move the Plot Ahead: Dialogue can guide the plot forward by revealing key details, conflicts, or situational changes. Crafting purposeful dialogue ensures that each conversation contributes to the narrative progression.

2. Characterization: Each character's dialogue style should reflect their personality, education, background, and emotional state. A well-written dialogue helps build and deepen character descriptions.

3. Realism and Engagement: Authentic, relatable dialogue can bring stories to life, making characters and situations more believable for the reader.

4. Indicate Time and Place: The vernacular, slang, and collocations used in dialogue can reveal a story's period and location.

5. Establish Mood and Tone: The tone of dialogue can help set the overall mood of the story. Conversations can be intense, humorous, casual, or confrontational, reflecting the emotional landscape of the narrative.

Remember that dialogue is not idle chatter or casual banter, but rather, a narrative device meant to serve one or more of these purposes.

## 15.2. Creating Authentic Voices

Dialogues give your characters a voice. Crafting distinct, believable voices for each character necessitates an understanding of their ages, backgrounds, education levels, and societal influences.

For instance, a sophisticated aristocrat from the 19th century will speak differently compared to a modern-day teenager. Factors such as culture, profession, and geographical location also influence how a character speaks. Achieving a unique voice for each character brings diversity and depth to your story.

Be consistent with the character's voice throughout the narrative. Inconsistencies can lead to reader confusion and disbelief. One effective method could be creating character sheets, noting attributes, quirks, and preferred expressions for each character, assisting in maintaining consistency.

## 15.3. Crafting Engaging Dialogue

Creating engaging dialogue is an art of balance. Conversational norms often involve mundane moments and tedious filler phrases, which can dilute the impact of your dialogue. As a writer, your job is to condense real-life conversation and extract its essence effectively.

Follow these guidelines for crafting engaging dialogue:

1. Be Direct: Begin the dialogue at the point of conflict or interest to engage the reader immediately.

2. Avoid Exposition: Resist the temptation to use dialogue for long-winded explanations. Show, don't tell, remains a cardinal rule.

3. Create Tension: Dialogue can be a useful tool in building anticipation, revealing secrets, or escalating conflicts.

4. Subtext Usage: Often, characters say one thing and mean another. Use subtext to reveal underlying emotions, hidden meanings, or contrast between a character's words and actions.

Remember, crafting dialogue is not just about what is said—it's also about what's unsaid. The intention behind the words, the pauses, the unspoken elements give the dialogue depth and meaning.

# 15.4. Focusing on Dialogue Mechanics

Dialogue mechanics – the rules and conventions – demand attention too. Proper use of punctuation, dialogue tags, and paragraph breaks are critical to maintain clarity and readability.

1. Use Punctuation Correctly: Dialogue should be enclosed in quotation marks, with punctuation marks inside the quotes. Each new speaker's dialogue should start a new paragraph.

2. Be Economical with Dialogue Tags: 'Said' is often enough. Overuse of descriptive tags like exclaimed, muttered, or gushed, distracts from the actual dialogue. Use action beats to break monotony.

3. Create a Dialogue Rhythm: Use a mix of long and short sentences, create pauses, build response lag for a more natural dialogic rhythm.

Subtle attention to these mechanics can dramatically elevate the quality of your dialogue, contributing to a rich, immersive storytelling experience.

## 15.5. Embracing Experimentation

Creativity and flexibility are essential components of crafting potent dialogue. Embrace new conventions, play with punctuation, or experiment with dialect-rich speech to bring forth innovative styles.

Be it experimentations with dialects as seen in Irvine Welsh's 'Trainspotting', or sparse, weighty dialogues in Cormac McCarthy's 'The Road', never be afraid to push boundaries and craft your unique dialogue style.

## 15.6. Final Words

Mastering the art of dialogue is a journey—one that requires constant learning, practice, and experimentation. Keep in mind, dialogue should always share the burden of storytelling. It should be interesting, carry weight, create conflict, and add depth to your characters. The right dialogue can enchant your readers, transporting them into your narrative universe, making them forget the world outside. Let your characters speak, express, argue, and engage in a dance of words. For, in that enactment lies the magic of storytelling.

# Chapter 16. The Magic of Metaphor and Simile

A shifting smokescreen, the scent on a breeze, or a storm within one's soul: the power of metaphor and simile is boundless. Crafted through linguistic alchemy, these linguistic devices transform the mundane into the magical, lending depth and color to the imagination's canvas. They are the tools that pry open new dimensions in storytelling, allowing us to delve into the human experience with an intimacy that direct description often lacks.

## 16.1. The Essence of Metaphor

Metaphor, a term stemming from the Greek "metapherein" meaning "to transfer," illuminates relationships, similarities and contrasts otherwise hidden in the folds of unadorned prose. It transposes features and qualities from one concept, the source, onto another, the target, thereby yielding an enriched understanding.

Consider the metaphor: "His words were shards of glass, cutting through her heart." It is not denoting the literal, physical characteristics of the words; rather, it uses the imagery of sharp, damaging shards to express the intense emotional harm they cause.

Highly malleable, metaphors don't abide by any rigid structure or configuration. They can be organized and adapted in a multitude of ways to serve your narrative vividly and specifically. They are divided broadly into two categories: explicit and implicit metaphors.

Explicit Metaphors are direct. They clearly state one thing is something else: 'Life is a rollercoaster.' They establish a one-to-one comparison, leaving little room for ambiguity.

Implicit Metaphors, however, are subtly woven into the text. Their magic lies in letting the reader decipher the hidden comparison. An example would be: "She sailed through life," wherein the metaphor is implied through the verb "sailed," comparing life to a journey on the sea.

## 16.2. The Spectrum of Simile

Similes are another potent weapon in a writer's arsenal. Derived from the Latin word "similis," meaning "similar," similes are explicit comparisons between two unrelated entities linked by common characteristics. Usually introduced with "like" or "as," similes help the reader visualize and understand complex ideas using everyday references.

For example, consider: "She was as unpredictable as a summer storm." The unpredictability of a storm is used to encapsulate the mercurial nature of her personality. Once again, it isn't about literal commonalities; it's about finding symbolic links that resonate with our shared human experiences.

Similes can be imbued with multifaceted layers. Overt similes simply state the comparison: 'She ran like the wind.' Subtler forms, like metaphoric similes, use metaphor within the comparison: 'His stare was like a wolf eyeing its helpless prey.' Inverse similes, another sophisticated form, leave the comparative aspect to the reader's imagination, providing only the context and the descriptive base: 'Her sorrow was like a dark cloud.'

## 16.3. Crafting Potent Metaphors and Similes

Crafting compelling metaphors and similes isn't about simply juxtaposing random imagery. They require a careful concoction of imagination, aptitude, and intuitive understanding of the reader's perceptions. Here are few strategies you can implement:

- **Seeking Familiar Ground**: Using familiar images, experiences, and concepts brings your metaphors and similes closer to the reader's personal understanding. The more your reader can relate, the more impactful your comparison.

- **Incorporating Sensory Details**: Engaging the reader's senses can dramatically improve the effectiveness of your device. When your comparison evokes the senses, it becomes a vivid experience rather than a dry observation.

- **Balance Precision & Flexibility**: While precise metaphors and similes can powerfully drive your point home, employing intentionally vague analogies allows readers to interpret the narrative based on their personal experiences.

- **Avoiding Cliches**: While some cliches are unavoidable, it's necessary to strive for originality. A unique metaphor or simile can pique the reader's interest, convey the intended meaning, depicting intricate emotions and situations in a refreshing way.

## 16.4. Metaphors and Similes: Weaving Context and Nuance

Creating a captivating narrative means more than just using metaphors and similes. Writers need to weave them seamlessly into the narrative, driving the story, building characters, setting, and mood.

Metaphors and similes can provide a stylistic shortcut to complex emotions or situations, offering readers a nuanced understanding of the character's experiences. For instance, "She had a heart like a desert," can suggest a character's emotional barrenness. Instead of explaining your character's traits, let metaphor and simile show your audience.

Consider also your setting: "The town was a forgotten painting," not only gives readers a visual of the town but also conveys a sense of desolation and neglect well-executed metaphors and similes can even set the mood, reinforcing tension, tranquillity, euphoria, or despair.

## 16.5. Conclusion: The Storytelling Power of Metaphor and Simile

Mastering the art of metaphor and simile is no small feat, but it's an endeavor worth undertaking. By illuminating abstract ideas with palpable comparisons, these literary devices invite readers into the heart of the narrative, transcending the limitations of direct expression. They are the strings that help weave a mesmerizing narrative tapestry, allowing readers to connect with the text on a deeper level. Whether you choose to wield them subtly or land a powerful visceral punch, remember to respect their magic. So, dear reader, as you navigate the labyrinth of storytelling, let metaphors and similes be your beacon, transforming your words into worlds.

# Chapter 17. Harnessing Imagination: The World-building Toolkit

Worlds exist within us - surreal landscapes, fantastical creatures, supernatural elements, or dystopian societies unfold like captivating illusions. Yet, it's not always an easy task converting these ponderings into solid, readable content that engulfs the reader's mind transporting them into the vistas we've created. Emulating the architects of awe-inspiring worlds, we'll take a page from their book to understand, hone, and apply the art of world-building.

## 17.1. Laying The Foundation

Before crafting intricate landscapes and weaving complex societal norms, we start with a basic skeleton - a seedling of your new world. This foundation may stem from a faint idea, a moment of inspiration, or an image that invigorates you. It could be a high-rise metropolis bathed in neon hues, a snow-capped mountain range guarding secretive tribes, or an intricately constructed bee-dominated society.

No corner is too obscure or concept too fantastical for your foundation to grow and flourish. It just needs to excite you, for your enthusiasm will fuel the construction of a detailed and fascinating world.

The fundamentals include the nitty-gritty of your world, like geographical layout, timelines, social structure, culture, religion, politics, and technology. These constitute the backbone of your world and integrate into the larger narrative, supporting, and complementing the plot and characters.

.Table: Fundamental Aspects
|====
|Aspect | Description

|Geographical Layout |The physical parameters:
landscapes, climates, landmarks.

|Timelines | Historical, present, and future events
marking the time flow.

|Social Structure | The societal hierarchy, norms, and
connections.

|Culture | Traditions, art, music, language, and other
cultural aspects.

|Religion | Belief systems, religious practices, deities
worshipped, rituals.

|Politics | Governance structure, political parties,
laws, rules, and regulations.

|Technology | Level of technological advancement,
innovations, and inventions.
|====

Remember, the level of detailing depends on your story's
requirements. While foundations remain crucial, not all
aspects need working out to the depths. Balancing
sufficient detail with the narrative requirements keeps
your world-building relevant and exciting.

=== Immersion Depths: Impeccable Detailing

Detailing breathes life into your world. Tiny specifics,

intricate touches, and thoughtful intricacies make the universe feel robust, immersive, and believable. It lends a touch of realism to the fantastical, encouraging readers to suspend disbelief and embrace your world wholly.

Bear in mind, every detail doesn't need a complex backstory or explanation. Tiny touches tend to paint a vivid picture. A peculiar aroma, a lingering sunset, an excessive display of wealth - such elements add substance, creating a fuller, richer, experiential world.

Creating exhaustive digital or physical world-building bible could assist you in gathering these details and reinforcing consistency.

=== The Art of Show Don't Tell: Seamless Integration

While detailing is fundamental, itⱺs equally vital to seamlessly integrate these details into the narrative. 'Show don't tell' forms the golden rule of storytelling and applies to world-building as well. Rather than explicit paragraphs describing the scenery, weave them into the story and character actions. Allow characters to interact with their surroundings, revealing the world piece by piece, eventually forming a comprehensive tapestry.

Avoid info-dumps - chunks of information abruptly placed, slowing down the narrative and stagnating reader's interest. Instead, strike a balance, sprinkle your world-building like seasoning, spreading out details throughout the narrative for maximum impact.

=== Fine-tuning Your World: Realism and Plausibility

Even the most magical world needs a fabric of believability stitched in. For this, laws underpinning your world - either confirming or refuting reality as we know it - play a primary role. For example, if your world includes magic, establish magic's boundaries, side effects, or costs to avoid making it a solution to every crisis and maintain suspense.

These laws lend reliability to your world, fostering reader attachment and mirroring the unpredictability of real life. They also foster conflicts, presenting plausible obstacles for characters to navigate, cultivating a captivating narrative.

=== Architecture of Cultures: Sociology and Anthropology

Peoples and cultures individualize your world, making it distinctive. Think about the social structure that prevails - is it a matriarchy, patriarchy, or an egalitarian society? Are there classes or castes? Societal norms and traditions lend texture to your world and reflect in character behaviors, dialogues, and actions. Remember to offer diversity, mimicking the range seen in our world, to engage readers in this societal tapestry.

=== Adorn With The Senses: Sensory Details that Enthrall

A reader doesn't inhabit your world with the mind alone—they experience it through senses, sight being just one element. Engage the senses of touch, smell, taste, and sound to fully immerse readers in your world. Describe the crunch of dead leaves, the stench of burning coal, or the numbing cold of the northern wind.

This exploration of sensual elements helps paint a richer portrayal, deepening the reader's connection to your fictional world.

=== Allowing Evolution: Dynamic World Building

Remaining open to evolution is crucial in world-building. As your narrative progresses, your world must mature, reflecting changes triggered by events or evolving societies. Considering this organic transience ensures your world doesn't stagnate but remains alive, breathing, morphing ▯ much like reality.

In conclusion, harnessing imagination for world-building is a journey in creativity, detail, and dynamism. It roots in your fascination, watered by the specifics you endeavor to construct. World-building is an art and a science, a dance between fantasy and believability, steadying on the tightrope of reader immersion. It's an act of creation and evolution deriving from your unique, unapologetic vision. As you proceed on this journey, embrace flexibility, marvel at the chaos, and allow yourself to build, unbuild, and rebuild. After all, a world exists for you to shape, and only your imagination sets the bounds.

== Destinies and Deadlines: Crafting Memorable Endings
A story, like all good things, eventually must come to an end. But what determines an ending as ▯good▯, as fitting, and most importantly, as memorable? Are endings truly the last impression of a story, or are they delicately woven threads that pervade the entire narrative, recognizable only when the final word is read?

=== The Essence of Endings

The art of crafting memorable endings begins with
understanding their nuanced importance. Endings do more
than just conclude a narrative; they reaffirm the
narrative journey, resonate lingering emotions, and
offer closure to readers. This requires an understanding
of not only the story but also the feelings, images, and
thoughts it inspired as readers traveled through its
narrative terrain. Understanding this, the significance
of endings can't be overstated—they bring thematic
closure, harmonize storylines, and resonate with readers
on a deeper level long after the book is closed.

=== Understanding Closure: Harmonizing Beginnings and
Endings

The quest for creating the perfect ending begins with a
look backward, toward the start of your narrative
journey. Every story, regardless of genre or form,
commences with a dramatic question--a catalyst for the
narrative journey that is to unfold. It may involve the
protagonist's quest for true love, the unraveling of a
complex mystery, or a grueling struggle for survival.

The ending in its most basic form is the resolution to
that dramatic question. It does not imply that every
loose end needs to be tied up perfectly; but the primary
thread (or threads) that drove the narrative should
reach a satisfactory solution. This doesn't always mean
a happy one—but one that feels complete and justified
within the context of the story.

=== Balancing the Expected and the Unforeseen

It's a fine line to tread between surprise and

fulfillment. Readers enjoy the unexpected; yet they also crave the satisfaction of their predicted endings. The key is a balance between avoiding predictability and not shocking readers with twists that make little narrative sense. To strike this balance, subtle foreshadowing woven throughout the narrative can serve to pave the way for the grand finale. Dropping hints to the possible outcome makes the ending feel logical—though not making it so clear that the outcome becomes predictable and unexciting.

=== The Echo Effect: Linking Endings and Beginnings

An underutilized yet powerful tool for crafting memorable endings is linking them to the story's beginnings—an artful technique known as the 'Echo Effect.' Symbolic resemblances, similar situations, or recurring images and phrases at the ending that echo back to the start can serve to highlight the growth and change the story and its characters have undergone. This kind of closure draws a full circle, creating an emotionally resonant and symmetry-rich ending.

=== Plot and Theme: Knotting the Threads

A truly satisfying ending seamlessly ties the plot's strands together while aligning with the story's underlying theme. It reflects the bigger picture: what the story was truly about beyond its plot. Achieving this symbiosis ensures the ending feels significant—not just an arbitrated situation but like a testament to the story's overall theme.

=== Power Punch: Ending with Strong Images or Emotions

A powerful tool for making endings linger in readers'

minds is concluding with strong, vivid imagery or
hitting a final emotional note. These emotional
impressions work on the subconscious mind, making the
narrative and its ending more memorable.

=== Death and Destiny: The Ultimate Endings

Two of the most memorable endings involve death or
destiny. While they may appear cliché, when used
carefully, they can lead to unforgettable closure.
Death, whether physical or metaphorical, can underline
the narrative's themes powerfully. In a similar vein,
destiny—whether it means fulfilling a prophecy or
realizing one's purpose—carries an enduring allure.

Rendered with care, precision, and a keen understanding
of the narrative journey, endings can echo in readers'
minds long after they've engaged with the story. They
offer a sense of completion, a resonant finish that
underscores and memorializes the narrative journey. But
remember, the ending is never truly the end—it's the
legacy your story leaves behind. It's what keeps the
narrative living, breathing, and influencing long after
it has been read.

== The Future of Storytelling: Digital Narratives and
Beyond
The wand of storytelling is forever poised on the brink
of the unexpected. It twirls and dances, tracing
patterns in the air yet to be seen, weaving tales yet to
be heard. It is not confined by time, nor does it shy
away from the unknown. Buckle up, for we are about to
venture into uncharted territories: The future of
storytelling.

It was not long ago when stories were harnessed within

the bindings of books, scribbled on scrolls, or
whispered in hushed tones around a flaming campfire.
However, the digital era has transformed the landscape
of storytelling, and the future holds exhilarating
prospects.

=== Digital Storytelling: More Than A Buzzword

In our rapidly digitized world, storytelling has found
new vessels and canvases. Digital storytelling refers to
the practice of using digital tools and media to tell
stories. Storytelling in the digital era is no longer a
solitary act. It is a dynamic and multimodal process
where creators, technologies, and audiences collide,
interact, and co-produce the narrative.

Interactive narratives, transmedia storytelling, and
augmented and virtual reality are examples of innovative
modes of digital storytelling. They exploit the
capabilities of digital technologies to engage the
senses and allow audiences to gain deeper, more
immersive experiences. A digital story can break the
fourth wall, enable personalization, and even adapt
based on user interaction.

=== Virtual Reality: Walk-In Narratives

Virtual Reality (VR) storytelling transports audiences
to a different space and time, weaving narrative threads
into a tapestry that surrounds and influences them.
Unlike traditional storytelling, VR narratives are
spatial and environmental, turning passive listeners
into active participants.

VR's locative storytelling potential offers untapped
possibilities for narrative immersion. Audiences may

walk around virtual realms, interacting with objects and characters, even influencing the storyline. With haptic feedback, simulated smells, or even tastes, a multi-sensory narrative that not just plunges audiences into stories, but engulfs their senses, is on the horizon.

=== Augmented Reality: A Layer of Magic

Augmented Reality (AR) adds a layer of magic onto our world, transforming everyday surroundings into interactive narratives. With AR, storytelling leaps out from digital screens into the physical world.

From scanning QR codes to reveal hidden tales, to embarking on location-based adventures with GPS-enabled devices, AR stimulates exploration and discovery. As our technologies evolve, personal, location-aware, non-linear narratives may become the norm.

=== Artificial Intelligence: The Co-Creator

Imagine a world where creative AI can understand the essence of good storytelling and imbibe it into their automated narratives. Algorithms have already begun crafting sports recaps, news articles, and even fictional stories.

Provided with a robust ethical framework, AI has the potential to evolve into a creative partner, recommending plot alternatives, devising character arcs, or brainstorming world-building details. However, caution should be adhered to protect against computational bias, maintaining originality and human connection.

=== The Social Media Canvas

Social media is a storytelling platform, a digital
canvas where millions sketch, paint, and etch their
narratives daily. Micro-stories unfold within Instagram
captions, vlog entries, tweets, or Facebook posts.

The line between creator and audience blurs in this
participatory culture, fostering an active, engaged
community. The future may see the rise of connected
narratives, where stories unfold across networks,
influenced by the collective storytelling prowess of
these online communities.

=== The Future Is Fluid

The future of storytelling is fluid and responsive. It
is a mirror lake whose reflections morph based on their
viewers. It is a concert where every instrument retains
its rhythm yet synchronizes in a harmonious symphony.

In this evolving narrative landscape, traditions and
technologies merge. Story wheel weaves with the digital
loom, tracing patterns from the past onto the cloth of
the future. But amidst these whirlwinds of change and
chaos, the magic must endure - the magic borne from
human connection and empathy. If the wand of technology
is waved with an understanding of the human heart, the
future tales will not just be told - they will be
cherished, remembered, and loved.

=== The Golden Thread

Amidst the tsunami of technology and the waves of
digital innovation, storytellers, listeners, writers,
and readers should not forget the golden thread that has
been weaving tales since the dawn of civilization: the

human connection.

Stories are effective because they connect us, bridge gaps, deepen our understanding of the world, and allow us to empathize with others. As we stand on the precipice of a new narrative era, let us remember to imbue our narratives, be they digital, interactive, or AI-aided, with the warmth and authenticity of human emotions.

That's the future of storytelling: a future where an ancient art form evolves, intertwines with technology, and yet, at the heart of it all, remains an endeavor steeped in humanity. Written words may fly faster with digital wings. However, their flight truly takes form when they touch minds, stir souls, dance in human hearts - for that's the home where stories were born, and that's where they will forever belong.